W9-CEG-265

Yellow Umbrella Books are published by Capstone Press
151 Good Counsel Drive, P.O. Box 669, Mankato, Minnesota 56002
http://www.capstone-press.com

Library of Congress Cataloging-in-Publication Data
Trumbauer, Lisa, 1963-
   Communities/by Lisa Trumbauer.
   p. cm.
   Includes index.
   ISBN 0-7368-0744-6
   1. Community—United States—Juvenile literature. 2. Community life—United States—
Juvenile literature. [1. Community life.] I. Title.
HM756.T78   2001
307'.0973   dc21   00-036472

Summary: Describes different types of communities, including cities, suburbs, and rural areas. Also discusses various occupations in a community.

Editorial Credits:
Susan Evento, Managing Editor/Product Development; Elizabeth Jaffe, Senior Editor;
   Charles Hunt, Designer; Kimberly Danger and Heidi Schoof, Photo Researchers

Photo Credits:
Cover: Unicorn Stock Photos/Aneal Vohra; Title Page: John Elk III (top left), Shaffer
Photography/James L. Shaffer (bottom left), John Shaw/TOM STACK & ASSOCIATES (top
right), Dan Krist/Pictor (bottom right); Page 2: International Stock/Stan Ries (top), Steve
Kahn/FPG International LLC (bottom); Page 3: John Shaw/Tom Stack & Associates; Page 4:
Gary Carter/Visuals Unlimited; Page 5: James Shaffer (top), John Elk III (bottom); Page 6: Scott
Barrow/International Stock (top), Unicorn Stock Photos/Jeff Greenberg (bottom), Page 7:
Visuals Unlimited/John Sohlden, Photo Network/Tom McCarthy (inset); Page 8: International
Stock/Scott Barrow (left), Mark Adams/FPG International LLC (right); Page 9: Visuals
Unlimited/M. Long (top), Unicorn Stock Photos/Aneal Vohra (bottom); Page 10: Visuals
Unlimited/Warren Stone (top), Dan Krist/Pictor (inset), Photo Network/Myrleen Ferguson
Cate (bottom); Page 11: Unicorn Stock Photos/Tom & Dee Ann McCarthy (left), Ed
Elberfeld/Pictor (right); Page 12: Unicorn Stock Photos/Paul Murphy (top), Photo
Network/Bachmann (middle), John Coletti/Pictor (bottom); Page 13: Index Stock Imagery
(left), Unicorn Stock Photos/D & I MacDonald (right); Page 14: Shaffer Photography/James L.
Shaffer (top), John Elk III (bottom); Page 15: Visuals Unlimited/A. Gurmankin (top), Visuals
Unlimited/Jo Prater (bottom); Page 16: Index Stock Imagery and/Bachmann

1 2 3 4 5 6 06 05 04 03 02 01

Communities

By Lisa Trumbauer

Consulting Editor: Gail Saunders-Smith, Ph.D.
Consultants: Claudine Jellison and
Patricia Williams, Reading Recovery Teachers
Content Consultant: Andrew Gyory, Ph.D., American History

Yellow Umbrella Books

an imprint of Capstone Press
Mankato, Minnesota

This is a city.

This is a suburb.

And this is the country.

How are these places alike?
They are communities!

Communities are places where people live.

This home is in the country. The country has a lot of open land. Neighbors live far away from each other.

This home is
in the suburbs.
The suburbs have
some open land.
Neighbors live
close together.

And this home is
in the city.
The city has very
little open land.
People have
many neighbors
all around them.

Communities have places
where people work.

This man lives
in the country.
He works
on a farm.

This woman
lives in the
suburbs.
She works
at a store in a
shopping mall.

This woman lives in the city.
She works in a tall office building.

Communities have people and places that meet our needs.

Doctors work at hospitals. They help us stay healthy.

Police officers help us follow the rules that keep us safe.

Firefighters
fight fires.
They also
keep us safe.

Postal workers work at post offices. They deliver mail from communities all over the world.

Librarians work at libraries. Librarians help us find information.

Communities have schools.
On the outside, schools may look
different.

But on the inside, all schools are
filled with teachers and students.
Teachers help students learn.

Communities have places where you can buy things.

You can buy clothes.

You can buy food.

You can buy other things you need.

Communities have places
where you go out to eat.

What do you like to eat
when you go out to eat?

Communities have places
to have fun!

Many
communities
have parks.

Many
communities
have movie
theaters.

How do people
have fun in your
community?

All communities have people!

Who are the people
in your community?

Words to Know/Index

Word Count: 295
Early-Intervention Levels: 13-16